TOO MUCH TONGUE

Adrienne Marie Barrios
and Leigh Chadwick

autofocus books
Orlando, Florida

PRAISE FOR *TOO MUCH TONGUE*

"In *Too Much Tongue*, Leigh Chadwick and Adrienne Barrios created a literary adventure forged in genuine friendship. These poems draw on the ordinary to deliver the transcendent. Like *Thelma and Louise*, but the highway is a wormhole through your heart."
—**Mark Leidner**, author of *Returning the Sword to the Stone*

"In *Too Much Tongue*, Adrienne Barrios and Leigh Chadwick carve out an unprecedented intimate space, one in which they are both separate entities and two halves of a singular voice presenting a startlingly accurate picture of our current human condition. These poems flit between hope and despair, yearning and satisfaction. They demonstrate what it might mean to stay sane during a global pandemic of illness and solitude. In this collaborative collection, Barrios and Chadwick are just like the rest of us—wandering into an endless dark with a flashlight, hoping that whatever we find is better than what we're trying to escape."
—**Taylor Byas**, author of *Bloodwarm*, Associate Editor of *The Cincinnati Review*

"*Too Much Tongue* reads like a psychological fairy tale in which two siblings navigate a forest of thoughts, uncertain as to whether they are lost or found—a journey into the psyches of wondering and wandering minds contemplating every meaning of existence. This collection of prose poetry is full of dreams and realities, where one blends into the other to cause a surreal state of beautiful sadness. There's a push and a pull between the narrators—sometimes a push and a push; others, a pull and a pull—and it's through these interactions that a quiet combustion occurs, giving us worlds upon worlds of light in all its variations. Both fierce and tender, *Too Much Tongue* is a gorgeous spectrum of words."

—**Shome Dasgupta**, author of *Tentacles Numbing*

©Adrienne Marie Barrios and Leigh Chadwick 2022
All rights reserved.

Published by Autofocus Books
PO Box 560002
Orlando, Fl 32856
autofocuslit.com

Prose Poetry
ISBN: 978-1-957392-11-0

Cover Illustration ©Amy Wheaton
Library of Congress Control Number: 2022946987

for A and L, my two favorite hearts
—LC

*for Leigh, who unlocked something
in me I may never fully understand*
—AMB

TOO MUCH TONGUE

These poems are taller mountains, broad-shouldered, bathed in Listerine, an empire of underwater cities. They are interstates shaped like amusement parks. The poems are stories, are emotions, are the first sweater on the first day of sweater weather as you walk along a shoreline, picking up shards of memories. Leigh Chadwick is ninety percent breath and that breath is the changing leaves on the trees in the town where you grew up. You are never not happy to visit her. You are always wanting to undress her. Adrienne Barrios is the clear water in the pond behind the house you never want to see again. She feels the way heartbreak sounds. Hail against your broken glasses. *Have you already lost your way?* Page fifty-seven of this book is the Krispy Kreme sign, flashing *warm*, twenty-seven minutes after waking up with a hangover. Page two is a soul gone dust. Page nine, an intimate climax dressed in semicolons, blushed gerund.

I

Adrienne Barrios can't get out of bed; her joints threaten cracks under the weight of being awake. Stuck there in bed with joints and thoughts, Adrienne Barrios considers the idea of missing someone she's never met. It's not a new idea. That doesn't make it less real. She asks Leigh Chadwick, *Do you ever miss the way someone says your name before you hear the sound of their voice?* and *Have you ever wondered where a mannerism is born?* Leigh Chadwick rests her head against a pile of beds, her daughter perched on top. Leigh Chadwick was born in the middle of a suburban sprawl. Her daughter, too. She looks at her daughter, perched on top of the pile of beds and wonders what makes a manner grow an *ism*. But she doesn't ask Adrienne Barrios. She doesn't ask her daughter or God or God's daughter or God's daughter's daughter. Leigh Chadwick wonders how *real* can be variable—what is *less* and what is *more*. Leigh Chadwick misses a good drug, the long sigh after a fresh fuck. She doesn't have to ask Adrienne Barrios if she feels the same.

Leigh Chadwick never knows what is or isn't a bed. Leigh Chadwick doesn't know where half of her veins go. Or what a spleen does. Or when Wikipedia became the bible. In the chapter after Deuteronomy, Adrienne Barrios has a dream. In her dream, all her teeth shatter. Adrienne Barrios shouldn't have been sleeping. *Get up,* the get up tells her. 10:12 p.m. on a Tuesday and Adrienne Barrios changes her dress but keeps her lipstick. Hell, she keeps her lips, too, along with that part of her neck she is always hoping you find. But for you to find it, you'd have to be real, and she isn't sure you sleep or eat or breathe or fuck or do anything people who are real do. Adrienne Barrios realizes she's talking about herself again. If she were Leigh Chadwick, Leigh Chadwick would say, *What isn't about yourself should be about yourself.* Adrienne Barrios asks Leigh Chadwick, *Do you think we're real?* and Leigh Chadwick doesn't answer, which is an answer.

Adrienne Barrios stands in line at the post office and wonders if she will ever stand in the last line at the last post office that ever exists. She is returning a package to Nordstrom—a shirt that would not fit three Adriennes put together. She thinks the word *sulfur* but doesn't know why. The man in front of her sweats gunpowder. She wonders what she would do if he pulled out a gun, any gun, and pointed it somewhere, anywhere. At her. Through her. Over her. Every preposition followed by her. She wonders if time would freeze before her heart gave out. Adrienne Barrios hates thinking about guns and would rather read a poem about Leigh Chadwick thinking about guns. Adrienne Barrios wonders if a bullet feels like a lie. She wonders if everything feels worse than a lie when coiled tightly, wrapped in metal, propelled through a spleen. She wonders if she should send Leigh Chadwick's daughter inside the box to Nordstrom, where everything is soft and cashmere and no one has guns. But she knows even this is a lie. Everything is a gun if you live long enough or are constantly squinting. Adrienne Barrios, who will never have kids, wonders how to keep

Leigh Chadwick's daughter safe. From bullets. From lies. From the bushes with the thorns. From tomorrow and every day after.

Whenever Leigh Chadwick leaves the house, she always forgets her better self at home. Adrienne Barrios thinks better selves are like soul mates. She doesn't have one. She wonders if she can order one off Amazon or if this is it. It's hard to tell these things and there's no one to ask. Last night Leigh Chadwick dreamt she was crushed by a pile of contributor copies. She spends the following afternoon trying to fit more poems into her poems while her daughter teaches race cars how to crawl. She sends a poem to Adrienne Barrios and asks, *Do you think this poem is a poem or a lie or the feeling of gravity on your shins?* Adrienne Barrios is too busy selling real estate on Reservoir Road to read the poem, but Leigh Chadwick doesn't mind. Leigh Chadwick understands there are bears and there are bears with claws and that every line goes somewhere even if it ends up nowhere. Leigh Chadwick is always the second *puff* in *puff, puff, pass.* Instead of getting an MFA, Leigh Chadwick asks the moon, *Do commercials ever make you cry?* A song goes, *When there is nothing left to burn, you have to set yourself on fire.* Leigh Chadwick pretends to be Leigh Chadwick. The lemonade has lost its melody. A piano is thrown against a wall. A bird is evicted from its birdhouse. A few blocks from Reservoir Road, a train stops on the tracks and says, *I don't think I can.* The moon goes deaf. The train packs up its coal and goes home.

Adrienne Barrios takes a Xanax and then she takes another. And then another. And then she pretends to sleep but instead she masturbates under the duvet and then she takes another Xanax but, shit, they're only .25 mg, so don't worry, she can take another. And another. And maybe she shares one or two with Leigh Chadwick, or maybe she fills a Pez dispenser with the white oval-shaped pills, and Leigh Chadwick opens her neck and the pills drop straight down into her stomach like pennies tossed into a wishing well. And maybe someday Adrienne Barrios and Leigh Chadwick stop taking Xanax. Instead maybe they take Valium or maybe they take Klonopin or maybe but probably not Ativan, or maybe they take a bed with a man shaped like a Xanax or Valium or maybe Klonopin or maybe the man is shaped like the sun or maybe the man is the sun because why not and so they decide to not take anything else. *No more*, Adrienne Barrios and Leigh Chadwick say. They go back to college and get doctorates in bird-watching because this is a poem, and what is a poem without birds, and what is a poem without Zofran, so Dr. Barrios takes a Zofran, and what is a poem without Adderall, so Dr. Chadwick takes an Adderall, and what is a medicine cabinet but a safe deposit box for emotions, and what is the corner of a room if you're not hiding in it, and what is a kitchen if the plates aren't cracked, chipped, left, sometimes swept into a pile, and what is a Xanax if it's not already swallowed?

II

Adrienne Barrios wonders if love is ever actually love or if it's just pretending to want to eat dinner together. She wonders if apple juice molds when no one is looking, or if she would hear the shatter of her windshield if she suddenly pulled the emergency break as she headed, during rush hour, eastbound on I-90. She wonders, *Would you still put the car away if all the parking spots became grass?* Someone tells Adrienne Barrios, *There are more than a few of us for whom life is an ache and a long red glare over the horizon.* Adrienne Barrios asks Leigh Chadwick, *Will you tell your daughter about the gravity of sadness, or will you hope she never needs to know?* Leigh Chadwick collects a single tear in a vial and mails it to 2053. 2053 doesn't mail anything back. 2053 is an asshole. Leigh Chadwick calls 2047 and says, *Can you believe 2053?* And 2047 says, *I know, but it'll never be anything worth remembering.* Somewhere, a rainbow forgets the color red. Somewhere, the wind goes purple. Somewhere, ginger forgets how to burn and you turn pale.

Leigh Chadwick has a sex dream about Pete Davidson. It's pretty good but not great. During her sex dream with Pete Davidson, Leigh Chadwick only bites her bottom lip a little. At the same exact moment, six states north, Adrienne Barrios has a sex dream about Leigh Chadwick having a sex dream with Pete Davidson. It's also pretty good but not great. During the sex dream about Leigh Chadwick having a sex dream with Pete Davidson, Adrienne Barrios doesn't bite her tongue at all, not even a little—Adrienne Barrios's teeth don't graze her skin once. She thinks, *Sometimes life promises more life, and sometimes life threatens more life,* though she doesn't know what that means. Outside is fresh snow and the crunch of Adrienne Barrios's boots as she wanders through tomorrow. Leigh Chadwick wants to text Pete Davidson that her favorite sexual position is all of them but in her sex dream with Pete Davidson, he didn't leave his phone number. Adrienne Barrios builds tidal waves in her bathtub while Leigh Chadwick walks into a wall to make sure she hasn't turned ghost.

Adrienne Barrios wakes with the words *simultaneous release* playing in her mind. She gets out of bed and puts on a pot of coffee. She wonders if sex is ever not just sex. She doesn't know why she keeps thinking about oxidized blood, but she doesn't care enough to figure out why. She calls Leigh Chadwick and asks who the first person was to yell the words *fuck me* or *harder* or *yes* and *oh God oh God* and *please please don't stop* during sex. Leigh Chadwick says, *If a poem falls in the woods, did I push it over?* Adrienne Barrios wonders if the first person knew they were the first person to yell the words *fuck me* or *harder* or *yes* and *oh God oh God* and *please please don't stop*. She thinks probably. She asks Leigh Chadwick and Leigh Chadwick says probably. Leigh Chadwick has never had sex while watching *Toy Story* but she still thought about Woody when her husband lost his hat and *oh*. If you were to do the math, nine months is nine months. Here is a fact: Leigh Chadwick has never touched anyone who has owned an empty medicine cabinet. And another: Adrienne Barrios has never touched anyone who has owned an empty medicine cabinet. Adrienne Barrios looks in her own medicine cabinet. It is full of nightmares and dreams and sometimes things stuck between the nightmares and dreams. Adrienne Barrios asks the razorblades in her cabinet if they sleep more the duller they get. She asks if the razorblades remember how skin sounds. Or the way her mother called her fat. Or the taste of vodka on lips already tasting of vodka. The razorblades don't answer. Adrienne Barrios asks Leigh Chadwick, *Do mothers hear razors, too?* Adrienne Barrios doesn't wait for the answer that Leigh Chadwick doesn't have. She doesn't want to know. Instead, she asks, *What do fathers hear?* Leigh Chadwick shrugs and Adrienne Barrios shrugs because no one knows.

Leigh Chadwick thinks about the last boy she kissed at a bar who wasn't her husband. It was eight years ago. His teeth were jagged, curled inside his mouth like a claw. She thinks about how when he opened his mouth she saw the jaws of life. Adrienne Barrios looks at her left wrist—naked except for the hint of vein under a freckle. She wonders when was the last time she wore a watch. A real watch. The cold metal clasp. The *tick tick tick*. She glides her index finger over the vein, the freckle, so light it could be bleached. She wonders when was the last time someone touched her wrist in a way that made her remember she had a wrist. She wonders if she still has a wrist.

In a state shaped like midnight, Adrienne Barrios decides to keep a shiv whittled from a crucifix in a hollowed-out Bible in the hidden netting that runs beneath her desk. She thinks, *Good cries are good, but they're always the ugliest.* She thinks, *Can you run out of tears?* In a state twenty-seven degrees warmer, Leigh Chadwick, over a commercial break during a rerun of *The Office*, licks some salt and kisses her husband who tries to keep her tongue. She tells him, *All the medicine cabinets in the world couldn't hold enough pill bottles.* She kisses him again. This time for the length of an infomercial. After, she lets him borrow her tongue for the afternoon. In a state still shaped like midnight, Adrienne Barrios looks out her living room window and watches the block walk around her. She says, *Eventually, if you go too far, you pass normal and cross back into abnormal.* She says, *And that's when the pills start to drip from your retinas.* Now, it's twenty-nine degrees warmer than the state shaped like midnight, and so Leigh Chadwick goes outside and waters her pill garden. If she had her tongue, she would say, *Have you ever collected*

PEZ dispensers? but it wouldn't matter if she had her tongue or not because there wouldn't be anyone around her to hear.

Leigh Chadwick buys a graveyard so she can say she bought a graveyard. Adrienne Barrios watches the morning dew graze the grass. Sometimes, Leigh Chadwick looks at a picture of herself and the picture of herself looks back. She thinks, *Sometimes most scenes are worth forgetting.* She thinks, *I have lost enough to know when to run toward an EXIT sign.* Adrienne Barrios used to let her hair down. Now, instead, she says things like, *It is so easy to fall asleep with a hand on your cheekbone.* And: *You don't need to say things to say things.* Leigh Chadwick has never touched a bear and she doesn't know why. Adrienne Barrios knows exactly why, though she doesn't tell Leigh Chadwick why. *Maybe a graveyard was a dumb thing to buy,* Leigh Chadwick says to Adrienne Barrios, but Adrienne Barrios isn't paying attention. She's daydreaming of chipped paint crested over her overalls as she stands at the top of a staircase where the boy she would later marry stands below, arms outstretched, ready to catch whatever may fall.

Sometimes, when Adrienne Barrios is peeing, she feels distinctly like she's dreaming. And sometimes, when Adrienne Barrios is dreaming, she almost pees, but she hasn't done that since she learned how to be embarrassed about the shape of a thigh. Now, she feels embarrassed about the shape of everything. Adrienne Barrios tells Leigh Chadwick, *I'm going to jump out a window if someone doesn't tell me where each gram goes when someone jumps out a window.* Leigh Chadwick says, *You jump out a window, I'll jump off a bridge.* Adrienne Barrios says, *Meet you at the bottom.*

III

Up out of the ground, out of nothing, a bottomless black pit looms and consumes and swallows Adrienne Barrios whole. Inside the pit, there is no way to find Leigh Chadwick. Adrienne Barrios can't see anything. She isn't sure where *a thing* begins and her body ends. Adrienne Barrios wonders if a bottomless black pit can ever develop a bottom, or if something molded can be salvaged or if it's always actually tainted, or if when you break someone's heart, do the cats feel it, too? Sometimes, Adrienne Barrios thinks she can still see the light, but she knows she's been falling for so long, she doesn't know which way is up.

Leigh Chadwick goes to a poetry reading and hides in a bathroom stall. She thinks, *Maybe I am home.* While hiding in the bathroom stall, she decides her favorite smell is soap—the pink kind, industrial, powder by the gallon. She thinks Adrienne Barrios would like it too. It's twenty minutes later and Leigh Chadwick is still in the bathroom stall, counting the squares of tile on the floor. Thirty-seven. The tile squares were once the color of a famous actress's teeth. Now, though, they remind her of a half-open bedroom door, a mattress on the floor, her lips pressed against your shoulder blade. Leigh Chadwick likes it here. She thinks maybe she'll stay.

Outside, all through Massachusetts, wispy snow blows sideways. Outside, metal scrapes the ground, but not often enough. Outside, as the minutes pass, over the course of hours, spread out over a whole day or maybe two, the snow piles up. The piles are soft. The piles sparkle. The piles are cold. Inside, Adrienne Barrios wonders if Leigh Chadwick's daughter has ever seen the snow, or if she would know what snow is, or if she's too young to think something cold can be beautiful, or if she would even care. Somewhere in Tennessee, Leigh Chadwick hands her daughter an ice cube. Her daughter sighs into the sun and drops the ice cube on the ground. The ice cube melts into a puddle. Leigh Chadwick wishes the puddle into a lake while, back in Massachusetts, Adrienne Barrios puts on a sweater made of smaller sweaters made of whatever makes mohair. Outside, a child cries. Outside, parked three streets over and two streets down, the car slowly disappears under a soft pillow of white as it is buried hemispheres deep.

On Fridays that feel like Fridays, Adrienne Barrios wonders if the people she calls friends also call people friends and, if so, do their friends call other people friends? Adrienne Barrios wonders if she is one of those people. Adrienne Barrios drinks whiskey out of a glass people drink whiskey out of and remembers a time when friends were real, when shoes went outside. When pizza looked like pizza. At the same time, a half-dozen states north, Leigh Chadwick drinks margaritas and thinks about sending a postcard to 2017. She imagines the word *treacle*. She wonders if she will ever grow wings. And at the same time, a half-dozen states south, Adrienne Barrios wishes she could walk through a field of Leigh Chadwicks and breathe the air in the field of Leigh Chadwicks and pluck the feathers off the just-hatched flowers in the field of Leigh Chadwicks. *Imagine,* Adrienne Barrios messages Leigh Chadwick. *Imagine people in a room filled with other people in a room.* Leigh Chadwick can imagine but only if she squints. This is what she tells Adrienne Barrios. Leigh Chadwick also tells her if you squint harder, an entire hospital empties and if you keep squinting until your eyes are nothing but skin, it is as if you've never slept in sorrow. Shortly after, a half-dozen states north, Adrienne Barrios wishes she could climb inside a martini and soak her pores until it dissolves her. Until it is impossible to tell where she starts and the martini stops. When Adrienne Barrios squints, she can see Leigh Chadwick in a field of Leigh Chadwicks. Adrienne Barrios squints harder and then someone is drinking her until she is nothing more than a drop of liquid and no one remembers her name. Even her name forgets her name.

On a Sunday in a month of Sundays, after spending a month of Saturdays watching HGTV, Leigh Chadwick drinks three mimosas at brunch and then builds a house out of popsicle sticks and horses. Inside the house, Adrienne Barrios tries on dresses that look like jazz clubs and martini glasses. She tries on a dress that feels like depression pretending to be lust. She picks a dress that makes her think of other dresses. Outside, Leigh Chadwick is outside. The inside of her head is damp. It matches her cheeks. They glisten, and Adrienne Barrios thinks Leigh Chadwick is the sun. Leigh Chadwick doesn't disagree. The sun shrugs. Leigh Chadwick remembers the sun before this one, and the one before that. It was a pretty good sun. Adrienne Barrios fills the house built out of popsicle sticks and glue with smaller houses made out of smaller popsicle sticks and miniature horses. The sun says it could fry an egg on pavement if it wanted. Leigh Chadwick doesn't disagree. Adrienne Barrios looks at her house holding the smaller houses. The heat begins to melt the glue. The popsicle sticks crack. The houses sway.

Every Wednesday at 12 p.m., Leigh Chadwick writes a letter to God. Every Wednesday at 12 p.m. when Leigh Chadwick writes a letter to God, the letter always starts with, *Haven't we all slept through a passive shooter drill?* God doesn't write back because maybe God always has a migraine every Wednesday at 12 p.m. or maybe God doesn't know how to read or maybe God's just an asshole. Leigh Chadwick wonders how many people die in hotel rooms and how many people sigh through bomb threats. She asks Adrienne Barrios, but Adrienne Barrios doesn't respond. She's busy wondering what the river remembers. Very little, she imagines. Everything is very little if you're always looking up. Every Wednesday at 12 p.m. when Leigh Chadwick writes a letter to God, she follows the sentence, *Haven't we all slept through a passive shooter drill?* with *When was the last time the sun was for sale?* Adrienne Barrios is still thinking about the river. She wonders if the ripples in the water are just the river having hiccups. Adrienne Barrios looks up. She wonders how many minutes in how many hours in how many days she spends looking up. She wonders if there is a kinder way to say that the girl fell off the top of the Hyatt Regency. Adrienne Barrios wonders if the girl got sick of thinking about things. Leigh Chadwick is sick of dreaming limericks. Adrienne Barrios is sick with. Leigh Chadwick nods the width of with.

IV

Adrienne Barrios tells Leigh Chadwick about the poem she was writing in the shower, but she can't remember any of the words, or any of the words that follow any of the other words. Adrienne Barrios says, *Something about listening with my eyes.* She looks at the mirror that Leigh Chadwick has crawled into. Leigh Chadwick says, *Do you think red lights ever get tired of constantly begging the world to stop?* Adrienne Barrios's new therapist says there's a twenty percent chance of feelings today. Leigh Chadwick spends the afternoon looking at the sky, playing hide and seek with the clouds. Adrienne Barrios's new therapist calls Leigh Chadwick and says, *Have you ever thought about how many parking lots it would take to make an elephant graveyard?* Adrienne Barrios packs up her eyeballs and moves to France where they dip their feelings in chocolate. Leigh Chadwick has never been to France, though she once watched a movie set in Barcelona. In the film, no one died, but two people kissed under a bridge. In the rain. The sound of a violin above them. Leigh Chadwick could never decide which was worse: *possibility* or the truth of what follows *next*.

Adrienne Barrios thinks about telling Leigh Chadwick that she plans to write a poem a day about writing a poem a day. Leigh Chadwick thinks about telling Adrienne Barrios that every song is a good song to dance to if you've just climbed off the mountain on your bed. Instead, Leigh Chadwick tells her, *I feel sleepy even when I'm not eating turkey.* As Adrienne Barrios thinks about the last time she climbed down the mountain on her bed, she writes a poem. This is that poem. Adrienne Barrios isn't sure what is and isn't a poem, and she knows Leigh Chadwick would say something like *you'll know it when you see it*, but she hasn't found that to be true. Adrienne Barrios asks Leigh Chadwick, *Do you know when a poem is a poem, or how cats know what a litter box is without anyone telling them?* Leigh Chadwick says, *Eighty-three percent of the time, I have no idea what I'm doing.* Adrienne Barrios says, *Eighty-three percent of the time, I have no idea what I'm doing.* Leigh Chadwick and Adrienne Barrios nod their heads, but not in unison. In a suburb in Boston or Memphis or Austin, another garage starts a band. A cat screams. A glass breaks or maybe a bird flies into a window. Leigh Chadwick and Adrienne Barrios notice the stains on their clothes. The stains are red and shaped like the wilderness. They don't know where the stains came from. They don't care enough to ask.

Adrienne Barrios sees the most beautiful person she has ever seen, and she wonders if beauty is finite. She wants to ask the most beautiful person she has ever seen if each time a cell flakes off and falls to the floor, does a star on the other side of a black hole weep? She wants to tell him, *You are only less beautiful when I blink.* She asks Leigh Chadwick, *Does beauty start at birth, or are we all imaginary?* Leigh Chadwick doesn't know how to answer questions that aren't about Leigh Chadwick. Adrienne Barrios spends the afternoon donating her emotions to charity while Leigh Chadwick adjuncts at the community college, teaching a course on how to sleep in sorrow. To drain weather. To scrape hieroglyphs off a cave wall. To waste the morning licking sweat off a chest. Adrienne Barrios tells the cashier at Wegman's that she is in love with love. Leigh Chadwick grows shoulders on her wings. Adrienne Barrios admits to her therapist that she has never driven a monster truck. Leigh Chadwick lets the ghosts tuck her into bed. Every night, she has a recurring dream where she is crushed by a pile of contributor copies. In the morning, while eating a bowl of Lucky

Charms, Leigh Chadwick reads an article in the *New York Times* that states the best way to not get shot by a bullet is to duck. Every morning Adrienne Barrios looks in her bathroom mirror and says, *Maybe I want to live forever.* She never knows which is more true, the *maybe* or the *want*.

Leigh Chadwick has a spine and she thinks that's weird. Leigh Chadwick has a spleen and she thinks that's weird, too. Leigh Chadwick has an orgasm and she thinks that's good. Across the street and six states north, Adrienne Barrios stares at a wall. The wall is beige. Or maybe eggshell. She should be able to tell, but she can't. She's too focused on the Ritalin she took, waiting for it to kick in, to make her blood become blood. Her eyes focus on a crack on the wall. The crack runs from the ceiling to the baseboard. Adrienne Barrios thinks the word *searing*. She asks Leigh Chadwick, *Can walls be walls if they can't promise to always be covered in paint?* Leigh Chadwick says, *Thoughts can be so simple. Like: what doesn't coo should coo.* Adrienne Barrios wonders what it would be like to coo. She gives birth to the panic that blooms inside a newly discovered mass grave. She feels teeth in her chest. She wonders how many times she can chew her own heart before it desiccates. She asks Leigh Chadwick if she feels the teeth, too. Leigh Chadwick says, *Yes, I feel the teeth. I have always felt the teeth.*

Sometimes, Adrienne Barrios thinks about gluing her mouth shut. She wonders if her mouth is glued shut, will her fingers still say things? If Adrienne Barrios glues her mouth shut, she can't ask Leigh Chadwick, *Why do so many women hate so many men but they don't want to empty the garbage themselves?* With Adrienne Barrios's mouth glued shut, Leigh Chadwick has to guess what Adrienne Barrios wants to ask. Leigh Chadwick says, *Are you thinking about the teeth again, or the way the sunlight glints of metal, or if your sweat tastes different after exercising on a Peloton?* Leigh Chadwick waits for the answer that never comes. Leigh Chadwick grows bored. Or maybe Leigh Chadwick grows so curious that she also glues her mouth shut. And with her mouth glued shut, she wonders if her fingers will still say things. Outside, a cat meows. Inside, the same. No one responds, not even Adrienne Barrios's fingers. Not even Leigh Chadwick's fingers. Somewhere, a garage door opens and a trash can is dragged to the bottom of the driveway.

Adrienne Barrios calls the non-emergency line and asks the doctor on call to please return her stomach. She wonders if she tells 700 more people she's fine, will she believe it herself? It's doubtful, she knows, but what in the world isn't doubtful? Leigh Chadwick asks Adrienne Barrios if the non-emergency line put her on hold. Leigh Chadwick says, *The last time I tried to return mine, I had to listen to Muzak for 18 hours and then the line turned casket.* Adrienne Barrios wonders where they put the phone line graveyard, or if phone lines are reborn as other phone lines, with other calls, carrying other voices. Adrienne Barrios's stomach reminds her of the point of a needle or knife or sword—take your pick, as long as it's sharp—driving through her organs. She takes four aspirin and holds her hand as she walks herself to bed.

Adrienne Barrios thinks about the effort it takes to walk from the living room to the kitchen, to twist her mouth into one expression after another. She asks, *If energy cannot be created or destroyed, will I run out before I can ever smile at my wrinkles in the mirror?* She thinks probably not. She can see the wrinkles already. Adrienne Barrios asks Leigh Chadwick, *Are wrinkles good or bad?* Leigh Chadwick says, *Yes.* That's enough for now. Leigh Chadwick catches the sun in a jar and puts the jar in a box she hides under her bed. She says, *Not yet.* She says, *Hold on for one more morning.* She says, *Let the sun bloom into a moment of stillness.*

Leigh Chadwick thinks bed is good. She says, *Bed is where people should be when they should be in bed.* Adrienne Barrios tries to nod with her head against a pillow robed in shimmering roses. She says, *Bed is where I go when I need to remember what it is to remember what it is to live.* Leigh Chadwick says something, but Adrienne Barrios can't hear over the marching band in her head. A cat tail swishes. A muscle spasms. Orange fur in the air, a dance, imperceptible. Something simmers. Someone creaks. A dim light dims.

V

Once again, Adrienne Barrios can't convince herself to get out of bed. She thinks about yesterday afternoon, the sleepiness of it, and the daydreams caught in thought bubbles floating above her head like cumulonimbus: *Could a person ever be too broken to be happy? And: What is the difference between* want *and* need *and does it matter? What could matter when even fire is on fire?* Adrienne Barrios pictures Leigh Chadwick, a few states west and several states south, scooping up her daughter in her arms, holding her close, smelling the top of her head, the innocence in her breath. Adrienne Barrios wonders if that love is the same as any other love. She thinks, *Probably not.* Adrienne Barrios wonders if her uterus still exists somewhere, or if it's decayed into nothing. She wonders if it matters when even the fire that's on fire is on fire. A few states west and several states south, Leigh Chadwick wonders if decay is always bad. Leigh Chadwick's daughter wonders when she can eat next. She wants to ask someone but she's still learning to build teeth. But she doesn't have to ask because Leigh Chadwick says, *You can eat now. And whenever you want.*

The baby naps while Leigh Chadwick crawls through an ellipsis. She stands in the middle of a cul-de-sac and wonders how many copies of this book it would take to chop down a tree. Adrienne Barrios wakes up in a mosquito net. Adrienne Barrios climbs out of the mosquito net and bombs a bath. A sign reads DEAD END. The baby is crying. Leigh Chadwick wonders what came first, the pyramids or the aliens. She wonders if she will ever stop wondering. Adrienne Barrios soaks in bits of lavender and sighs. She is tired of her panic attacks inviting their panic attacks over for dinner. Neither Leigh Chadwick nor Adrienne Barrios can remember who wrote the line, *Who can afford happiness in this economy?* Or: *My dreams never make it past Go.* Even so, they find themselves lost in the sincerity of breath. The magic of a pill. The fear of age. The dream of starlings.

Leigh Chadwick listens to "Step" by Vampire Weekend while driving to the Orange Hat. She's two miles south of Clinch River when she sees the bluest bird. She doesn't know its name. Leigh Chadwick asks Adrienne Barrios, *What is the name of the bird so blue it is a pastel that has been given wings?* Adrienne Barrios tells her there is no name, that it is known as the only thing in this world that wasn't a mistake. Leigh Chadwick disagrees. Leigh Chadwick can think of at least one more thing that wasn't a mistake. That sometimes mistakes are mistakes, and other times, mistakes are life itself—all curly tops and orange blossoms and record players. After finishing "Step," Leigh Chadwick puts on "Lua." The sun can't tell if it wants to set. Adrienne Barrios never knows when it's time to get ready for bed. She never wants to disappear until it's too late.

Adrienne Barrios wonders if Leigh Chadwick's daughter will ever read these poems and feel the way a coyote feels when returning to its den after a long hunt, or if she'll think, *Who the fuck is Adrienne Barrios,* or if she'll feel nothing at all. Leigh Chadwick says, *The future makes me sad.* Adrienne Barrios asks, *Is there a time that doesn't make you sad?* Leigh Chadwick says, *No.* Then, *Yes.* She says, *That time my husband climbed into the base of my spine and for three mornings in a row I woke up with sunshine in my veins.* Adrienne Barrios and Leigh Chadwick both look at Leigh Chadwick's daughter. They see that she glows. They take her out into the yard and she is the second sun. She grows a halo where halos were always meant to grow. The day quiets. For exactly twelve seconds, no one pulls the trigger of a gun. The sun sighs. Leigh Chadwick's daughter sucks her thumb as her halo turns tangerine. Leigh Chadwick wonders how anyone can have children and make it out alive—if anyone can have children and stay soft.

Adrienne Barrios thinks Leigh Chadwick into an old movie where life is simple and kids play happiness and husbands pretend fidelity more convincingly than they do now. But that's a lie. Leigh Chadwick ties her apron tighter around her waist and sweeps sadness into a dustpan. She drinks anxiety. Her makeup falls into the garbage disposal. Adrienne Barrios wants to say something but she doesn't know the point—when was the last time anyone listened to a middle-aged woman? Leigh Chadwick says, *What age do you start thinking about age?* Adrienne Barrios shrugs. Leigh Chadwick sweeps disappointment into a dustpan. The collective sound of matches on matchbooks to light infinite cigarettes causes heart attacks across the country. A threaded seat belt snaps a bridge in half. Leigh Chadwick turns off the lights. A forest fire yawns. A red dot smolders.

A cigarette causes a fire which causes a cliché. The smoke alarm is making the living room cough. Adrienne Barrios hears footsteps in her teeth. She doesn't remember where she put Leigh Chadwick or what it means to breathe, or how it feels to taste, or why anything matters. What she does know: even flames have their own flames. And: even a neighborhood charred is still a neighborhood. The firefighters are interviewing the lack of rain. *When did brilliance forget how to weather?* the firefighters ask. *The day we went on strike,* the weather says. Adrienne Barrios sits on the sidewalk and watches the flames lick the windows. She checks her pocket and finds Leigh Chadwick sleeping inside a memory. She wonders how many Leigh Chadwicks have fallen asleep inside how many memories. She imagines many, maybe too many, though how many is too many she doesn't know. She looks at her hands, her fingers. She wonders why there are only ten of them and how many things you can't count with your fingers because there are only ten. *Too many,* Adrienne Barrios imagines. She thinks about the flames, and the smoke, and the dreams that will never be dreamt. They are uncountable. Adrienne Barrios feels small, too small—a pebble stuck inside her shoe, a mistake with the boy who liked her bangs, every year that will follow—and then the moment ends and what is left but for Leigh Chadwick to climb out of a pocket and walk into a star.

Adrienne Barrios steps out of Leigh Chadwick's brain. Adrienne Barrios looks around at the bullet casings and the holes in the trees and the bodies gone to wherever gone goes and the empty pill bottles and the feathers and the thoughts and prayers and the magazines filled with other magazines. What is a word but a word? Adrienne Barrios decides she likes it better in Leigh Chadwick's brain, so she climbs back inside. She curls up next to Leigh Chadwick's amygdala and whispers, *Every reality is made up of a million other realities, and nothing is real but you.* Leigh Chadwick lets out the breath she's been holding since they invented anxiety and says, *The world would be better if more people held boomboxes over their heads,* and a bird flutters and a child smiles and someone holds a hand and the hand is sweaty but the someone wants to hold the hand anyway and all the medicine cabinets stay closed and perfectly still and the word *forever* is on a lip stuck to another lip and nothing else ever needs to be said and

Acknowledgements

Adrienne Barrios and Leigh Chadwick would first like to acknowledge Leigh Chadwick's daughter, because they would be nowhere without her: she is the sun and the guiding light; she is the one worth saving; she is the embodiment of what the future might be. Adrienne Barrios would also like to acknowledge Leigh Chadwick, without whom none of this would have started, but then, of course, Leigh Chadwick reminds Adrienne Barrios that none of it would have continued without her, either. They both nod. They would like to acknowledge themselves individually, too.

Here is where Leigh Chadwick says that Adrienne Barrios is being too modest, because Leigh Chadwick is certain that this book would not have become a book if Adrienne Barrios weren't Adrienne Barrios. But most importantly to Leigh Chadwick, she is grateful of the friendship that has come from the time spent working on this book. These words are important and very good (obviously), but words are never as good as other people.

Adrienne Barrios and Leigh Chadwick would be remiss if they didn't profusely thank the journals that published poems from this collection, including *Passages North, Autofocus Lit, trampset, No Contact, The Bear Creek Ga-*

zette, The Leigh Chadwick Review, Five South The Weekly,, South Florida Poetry Journal, JMWW, Bending Genres, and *Bullshit Lit Anthology I.*

Adrienne Barrios would like to thank the post office on Beacon St. for the continued inspiration while standing in line. Leigh Chadwick remembers that poem; it was one of the first. She also thanks the post office. Leigh Chadwick would like to thank the gas station down the street and a few blocks over where she regularly had a few minutes to think, which is key to being alive. She would also like to thank the Notes App on her iPhone, in which large chunks of this book were written. Adrienne Barrios also thanks her Notes app. They'd both like to thank Twitter and Google Docs. They'd both especially like to thank Xanax, as well as the occasional Valium.

Leigh Chadwick and Adrienne Barrios also both agree that, above all else, they owe an immense gratitude to Michael Wheaton, who saw what this collection could be and allowed it to be, first and foremost, true to itself. They will forever be grateful for his generosity, open mind, kind heart, and enthusiastic spirit for the authentic and the unfiltered.

Finally, Leigh Chadwick and Adrienne Barrios would like to thank you, the reader, for spending your time with them. They know there are so many other places you could have been than here.

About the Authors

Adrienne Marie Barrios is autistic and has an extensive collection of vintage and vintage-reproduction dresses, shoes, sweaters, accessories, and bone china teacups that she actually drinks from. Adrienne Marie Barrios is editor-in-chief of *Reservoir Road Literary Review* and *CLOVES Literary.* In addition to being co-author of *Too Much Tongue*, Adrienne Marie Barrios is the author of her debut solo collection *We Don't Know That This Is Temporary* (Redacted Books, 2023). Adrienne Marie Barrios's work has appeared in numerous journals, including *trampset, Passages North, Rejection Letters, Stanchion Zine, and HAD,* among others, and she has been nominated for a Pushcart Prize and Best Microfiction. Adrienne Marie Barrios edits award-winning novels and short stories and is currently at work on both of those very things and so much more. Adrienne Marie Barrios can be found online at adriennemariebarrios.com.

Leigh Chadwick is the author of *Your Favorite Poet* (Malarkey Books, 2022) and *Sophomore Slump* (Malarkey Books, 2023). Leigh Chadwick's poetry has appeared in *Salamander, Hobart, Passages North, Pithead Chapel, The Indianapolis Review,* and *No Contact,* among others. Leigh

Chadwick is the executive editor of Redacted Books and is a regular contributor at *Olney Magazine,* where she conducts the "Mediocre Conversations" interview series.

Leigh Chadwick is currently at work on a novel. Leigh Chadwick can be found online at leighchadwick.com.

—also from—
Autofocus Books
[2022]

Duplex - Mike Nagel
XO - Sara Rauch
Until It Feels Right - Emily Costa
Cleave - Holly Pelesky
Nextdoor in Colonialtown - Ryan Rivas

find them at
autofocuslit.com/books

CPSIA information can be obtained
at www.ICGtesting.com
Printed in the USA
LVHW042137301122
734375LV00020B/299